Native Americans

Table of Contents

Thematic Units

More Activities and Ideas

Reproducible Activities

Save time and energy planning thematic units with this comprehensive resource. We've searched the 1986–2000 issues of **The MAILBOX**® and **Teacher's Helper**® magazines to find the best ideas for you to use when teaching a thematic unit about Native Americans. Included in this book are favorite units from the magazines, single ideas to extend a unit, and a variety of reproducible activities. Use these activities to develop your own complete unit or simply to enhance your current lesson plans. You're sure to find everything you need for strengthening student understanding of our first Americans.

Project Manager: Leanne Stratton
Copy Editors: Sylvan Allen, Gina Farago, Karen Brewer Grossman, Karen L. Huffman, Amy Kirtley-Hill, Debbie Shoffner
Cover Artists: Nick Greenwood, Kimberly Richard
Artist: Jennifer Tipton
Typesetters: Lynette Dickerson, Mark Rainey

President, The Mailbox Book Company™: Joseph C. Bucci
Director of Book Planning and Development: Chris Poindexter
Book Development Managers: Stephen Levy, Elizabeth H. Lindsay, Thad McLaurin, Susan Walker
Curriculum Director: Karen P. Shelton
Traffic Manager: Lisa K. Pitts
Librarian: Dorothy C. McKinney
Editorial and Freelance Management: Karen A. Brudnak
Editorial Training: Irving P. Crump
Editorial Assistants: Terrie Head, Hope Rodgers, Jan E. Witcher

www.themailbox.com

©2002 by THE EDUCATION CENTER, INC.
All rights reserved.
ISBN# 1-56234-500-1

Thematic Units...

from The MAILBOX® magazine

NATIVE AMERICANS
OF THE PACIFIC NORTHWEST

Towering totem poles, jumbo canoes, and elaborate celebrations are all part of the rich culture of the Native Americans who made their home in the Pacific Northwest. Use the following activities and literature suggestions to supplement an investigation of truly remarkable people. *ideas contributed by Stacie Stone Davis*

TEACHING TIPS

As you prepare to teach about Native American people and their cultures, remember that good information, common sense, thoughtfulness, and sensitivity are your best guides. Always differentiate between the past and the present. Avoid activities that perpetuate stereotypes, such as role-playing or the choosing of "Indian" names. Constantly ask yourself how you are increasing your students' knowledge of these rich cultures and ways of life. And always respect the sacred nature of objects and practices associated with Native American cultures. If you are unsure if an activity is appropriate, the best thing you can do is consult a Native American for advice.

PICTURING THE PACIFIC NORTHWEST

The Native Americans of the Pacific Northwest lived in the narrow band of coastal land that stretches from the southern tip of Alaska to northern California. The mild, moist climate made the region one of dense mists, lush evergreen forests, abundant vegetation, and numerous game animals. Rich freshwater fishing and a variety of sea animals provided most of the food supplies, while huge trees furnished the people with materials for tools, clothing, transportation, and shelter. Enlist your youngsters' help in locating the Pacific Northwest region on a U.S. map. Describe the climate and natural resources of the area, and ask students to contemplate how these elements may have affected the day-to-day lives of the Native Americans who lived there. Follow up the class discussion by having students complete the reproducible activity on page 9. The picture is clear: the environment of the Pacific Northwest greatly influenced the lifestyles of the Native Americans who lived there.

"TREE-MENDOUS" TRANSPORTATION

Canoes, carved from large cedar trees, were the basic method of transportation in the Pacific Northwest. An ocean-going canoe might measure more than 60 feet in length and hold more than a dozen men! To give students an idea of the size of these king-size canoes, take them into the hallway and have them sit in a straight line—one behind each other. Invite youngsters to estimate if the line they have formed is longer than, shorter than, or equal to 60 feet. Then place a length of masking tape near the front of the line, and use a tape measure to measure the length of the students' line and a distance of 60 feet. Place a second piece of masking tape at the latter location. Next discuss possible seafaring scenarios with your students: from riding out a rough storm in a 60-foot canoe to paddling it for hundreds of miles to keeping the canoe upright during the capture of a 200-pound halibut! Then take a class vote to find out how many students are eager to set sail in a huge hollowed-out log!

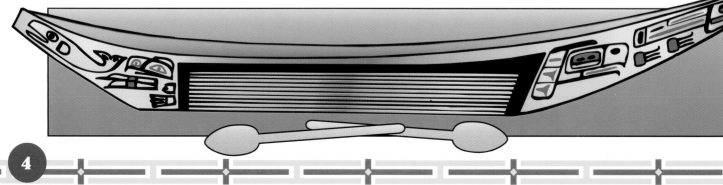

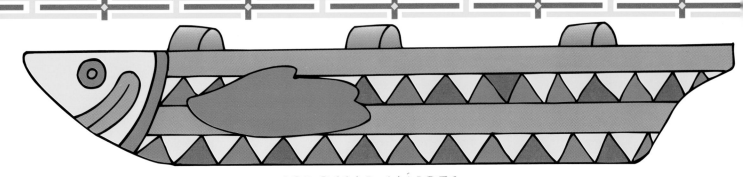

COLOSSAL CANOES

In addition to transportation, the canoe was used for fishing, whaling, trading, *potlatches,* and war. It was not uncommon for native groups to make different kinds of canoes for different purposes. The most impressive canoes were the ceremonial ones that were used for war or potlatches. Have each student make and decorate a colossal canoe for a specific purpose.

To make a canoe, cut away each side panel of a large, brown paper grocery bag; then fold the resulting length of paper lengthwise and trim each end of the paper to create a desired canoe shape. Next flatten the cutout, and use colorful paints to decorate the cutout with symbols or illustrations that tell a story. When the cutout is dry, refold it, and either staple or glue the ends to form the canoe. Cut crossbars from the remaining paper scraps and glue them inside the canoe. Set aside time for each child to present her colossal canoe and tell its story. Then display these vessels around your classroom or in the school library.

VERY BIG HOUSES

The peoples of the Pacific Northwest built massive wooden houses that were even more impressive than their canoes! Each permanent multifamily home measured at least 40 feet by 30 feet. There were no windows and only two small openings: one in the roof for smoke to escape and one at the front of the home. The front entrance may have been part of an elaborately carved and decorated doorway post. To give students a feel for the largeness of these homes, arrange two 30-foot and two 40-foot yarn lengths to form a large rectangle. Ask your entire class to sit inside this rectangle and imagine living in a structure this size with 40 or more family members. Explain that inside the home, woven mats partitioned off each family's living quarters. Each living space opened into the center of the home where fires for heat, light, and cooking were kept burning. Ask students to discuss what they think the advantages and disadvantages of this lifestyle might be. Then see "Under Construction" for a home-building project.

UNDER CONSTRUCTION

Building a wooden house was often an elaborate process marked by ceremonies and feasts. Have your students enlist the help of their family members in getting started on this home-building project. In a letter to parents, ask that each child bring to school a box with a removable lid, such as a shoebox. For easy management, request that the box and its lid each be wrapped with brown paper and that a small hole (about one-inch square) be poked in the center of the wrapped lid. When you have a wrapped box and lid for every student, celebrate with a few extra minutes of recess or free time.

For the next stage of construction, have students complete the interiors of their homes. Provide tissue paper for making flames and brown paper for making partitions. Plan another celebration when this stage of construction is complete.

Finally have each child complete the exterior of his home. To do this, he draws planks on the outside walls and the roof. Next he designs, colors, and cuts out a poster-board doorway post and attaches it to the front of his house. To complete the roof, he glues overlapping paper strips (planks) and small rocks to the lid. Encourage each child to share a fact or two about the home he constructed before putting these projects on display.

WOODEN WONDERS

Nearly everything in the village was made from wood. That included houses, totem poles, canoes, dishes, ceremonial masks—*and* clothing! How was clothing woven from wood? First a section of outer bark was carefully removed from a cedar tree; then the soft inner bark was cut into long strips. Back in the village, this bark was soaked, beaten into soft shreds, and prepared for weaving. A popular hat of the region, called a *spruce root hat,* was woven using the roots of a spruce tree that were heated and then prepared in a similar way.

Students will enjoy making these mock spruce root hats. To make a hat, cut away the center portion of a nine-inch paper plate, leaving only the plate's rim. Place the rim over an inverted 16-ounce Chinet bowl; then staple the rim to the bowl as shown. Use crayons or markers to decorate the hat.

A TASTE OF THE PACIFIC NORTHWEST

For the Native Americans, salmon was by far the most important fish of this region. To show their respect and appreciation for the bountiful fish, the bones of the first salmon of the year were returned to the river where the fish was caught. This first salmon, called *Chief Salmon,* was honored in prayer and song in hopes that the salmon would return to the same river the following year. Add some flavor to your study of the Pacific Northwest by giving each student a portion of cooked salmon atop a cracker. Since berries were also an important part of their diet, consider serving a few fresh berries too. Or, if you're a bit more adventuresome, bake a berry cobbler for your students to sample. Yum!

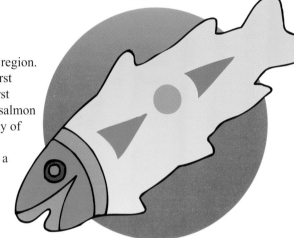

TOWERING TOTEM POLES

More than any other item, the *totem pole* is the symbol of the Pacific Northwest. Unfortunately many totem poles were destroyed when missionaries who moved into the area believed that the Native Americans worshipped the poles. This was not the case. The poles—which portray some animals, birds, fish, heavenly bodies, and prominent landmarks—symbolize the highlights of a family's ancestral history. Help students learn more about these awe-inspiring art forms by reading aloud the photo-illustrated book *Totem Pole* by Diane Hoyt-Goldsmith (Holiday House, Inc.; 1994). Then, as a follow-up to the book, have each child bring to school an empty (and clean) 16-ounce can for a totem-pole project.

To begin, divide your students into groups of four and assist each group in taping its four cans together so that the closed ends are exposed. Next have each group wrap a 12" x 18" sheet of tan construction paper around its project, securely tape the paper in place, and lay the project down so that the paper seam is at the back.

Explain that each child in the group will decorate one-fourth of the project to symbolize an important event of his life. Then give each child a four-inch square of blank paper on which to draw his idea. Remind the class that actual totem-pole carvers draw their ideas on paper first too. When the group has agreed on the placement of each child's contribution, each member of the group uses construction paper and/or markers to decorate his portion of the pole.

Plan to raise these poles at a class potlatch (see page 7). Or have each group in turn raise its totem pole for the class; then ask each child in the group to say a few words about his contribution.

FUN AND GAMES

One of the greatest advantages of living in the Pacific Northwest was the availability of food. Because the Native Americans living there could gather a year's food supply between May and September, they had more time during the rest of the year for fun and games. Your students will enjoy playing these two games that have been passed down from Native Americans of the Pacific Northwest.

Just for Laughs: Played by both adults and children, the object of this large-group game is to make the opponent laugh! Divide the class into two equal teams: A and B. Ask one student from each team to come to the front of the classroom. On your signal, the player from Team A has 15 seconds to make the player from Team B laugh. There may be no physical contact. If she succeeds, she earns one point for her team. If she does not, the opposing team earns one point. Then the roles are reversed. When this round is over, select two more opponents. Continue play in this manner until each player has taken at least one turn. The team with the most points wins the game!

How Many Groups?: This guessing game is great for small groups. One player is It and is given 20 or more small sticks (or dried beans or pasta). The remaining players close their eyes tightly while It arranges the sticks in a series of groups on the ground. When It calls "Ready!", the other players—keeping their eyes closed—guess how many groups of sticks were formed. The first player to guess correctly becomes the next It.

PAM CRANE

SHARING THEIR CULTURE

Native American culture is an important part of our country's past and its future. Explain to students that *traditions* in every culture must be passed along from generation to generation to avoid being forgotten. Ask students to describe traditions that their families practice; then help them realize that one day they will pass these traditions on to a younger generation. An excellent example of this transfer of information is described (and photographed) in *A Story to Tell: Traditions of a Tlingit Community* written by Richard Nichols (Lerner Publications Company, 1998). In this story, a modern-day Tlingit grandmother shares the history and traditions of her people with her 11-year-old granddaughter. By the conclusion of the book, your youngsters—like her granddaughter—will be more knowledgeable about Tlingit culture and traditions, and they will have a much better understanding of the importance of sharing knowledge with others.

A PACIFIC NORTHWEST POTLATCH

A *potlatch*—a Chinook word meaning "to give"—was an enormous feast held by a family group or *clan* to honor another clan. Most potlatches were held during the winter when there was very little other work to be done. The purpose of the potlatch was to confirm a clan's social status and show their wealth. To accomplish this, the host clan showered their guests with food. They also gave each visitor (often totaling several hundred) a gift ranging from a cedar-bark blanket to a canoe! It often took years to prepare for a potlatch, partly because so many gifts needed to be made.

As a culmination to your study of peoples of the Pacific Northwest, hold a variation of the traditional potlatch. For this classroom celebration, have your students share their *wealth of knowledge* about the Native Americans of the Pacific Northwest with their family members. Plan for students to share the projects they've completed during their study, along with additional facts they've learned about the native peoples of this region. Then—after a snack of berry cobbler, crackers and salmon dip, and springwater—read aloud one or more of the literature suggestions reviewed on page 8. Now that's impressive!

STORIES TO SHARE

TALES FROM THE PACIFIC NORTHWEST

The native peoples of the Pacific Northwest were extremely gifted storytellers. From their tales emerged the character and spirit of a communal people living in constant awareness of the world around them. Rich with wisdom, fundamental values, and an utmost respect for nature, their stories and variations of them continue to teach today. Use this sampling of folklore to promote a better understanding of a most respected culture.

By Deborah Zink Roffino

COYOTE AND THE FIRE STICK: A PACIFIC NORTHWEST INDIAN TALE

Retold by Barbara Diamond Goldin & Illustrated by Will Hillenbrand
Gulliver Books, 1996

Proud Coyote agrees to help the People by bringing them warmth and light. With the help of his sisters, he contrives an elaborate plan to steal Fire from the evil ones at the top of the mountain. Playful illustrations transport a relay team of fire-carrying animals down the rugged peak. It's a group effort until the very end—when clever Coyote retrieves Fire from a tree *and* takes full credit for the entire fire-stealing event.

THE EAGLE'S SONG: A TALE FROM THE PACIFIC NORTHWEST

Adapted & Illustrated by Kristina Rodanas
Little, Brown And Company; 1995

In a place edged by mountains and shoreline, a separated people learn how to become a village, celebrate their gifts, and be thankful—all because of one small boy. Guided by the wisdom of an eagle-man and his ancient mother, the boy uses his artistic sensitivity to unleash a new spirit of togetherness. Intense illustrations with mesmerizing detail capture the cool colors of the Pacific Northwest.

STORM BOY

Written & Illustrated by Paul Owen Lewis
Beyond Words Publishing, Inc.; 1995

In this simple tale, a young Haida boy is thrown from his canoe during a violent storm and finds himself in a strange, exotic land under the sea. Here—in a land of largeness—he comes to understand the importance of cultural exchange. Vivid paintings brighten the pages and provide culturally significant details. An informative note from the author supplies additional insight into the culture and art of the native peoples of the Pacific Northwest Coast.

FROG GIRL

Written & Illustrated by Paul Owen Lewis
Beyond Words Publishing, Inc.; 1997

Written as a companion story to *Storm Boy,* this dramatic account of a young girl's efforts to save the Frog People from an erupting volcano can easily stand alone. Well-written text and powerful artwork promote the importance of mutual respect among all living things. Superb, faithful renderings of totem poles with traditional exaggerated features will fascinate and inspire students. An author's note at the book's conclusion furnishes fascinating details about the story.

Name_____

PICTURE THIS!

Color and cut out the five pictures.
Read each clue below.
Put a drop of glue on each •.
Glue the matching picture in place.

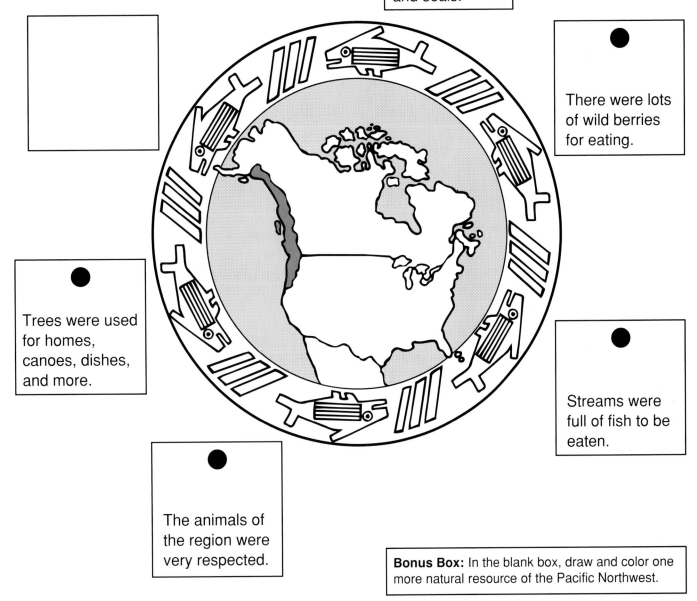

The ocean was a source of sea otters, whales, and seals.

There were lots of wild berries for eating.

Trees were used for homes, canoes, dishes, and more.

Streams were full of fish to be eaten.

The animals of the region were very respected.

Bonus Box: In the blank box, draw and color one more natural resource of the Pacific Northwest.

Note to the teacher: Use this page with "Picturing the Pacific Northwest" on page 4.

9

Native Americans of the Southwest

For countless centuries the beautiful, yet harsh land of the Southwest has been home to many different groups of Native Americans. Use the following activities and literature suggestions to supplement your investigation of these remarkable desert dwellers.

ideas contributed by Stacie Stone Davis and Charles J. Wohl

Surveying the Southwest

The Southwest stretches throughout Arizona and New Mexico and into southern Utah and southwestern Colorado. With your students' help, locate this region on a U.S. map. As you and your students investigate the area, reveal that it is home to the vast Grand Canyon, the colorful Painted Desert, the rugged Sangre de Cristo Mountains, the red sandstone buttes and mesas of the Monument Valley, the saguaro-cactus forests of the Sonoran Desert, and much, much more. Show students photographs of the area from assorted resource books and ask them to speculate about the day-to-day struggles of living in this area long ago. Then challenge students to be alert for signs of how the environment of the Southwest influenced the lifestyles of the Native Americans who settled there.

A Meaningful Matrix

Native Americans have lived in the Southwest for thousands of years. Scientists have learned much about their complex and rich lives by studying both the past and the present. As students discover information about the past living conditions of specific Native American groups, record it on a matrix like the one shown. Use the gathered information to help students identify and better understand the similarities and differences among the Native American groups of the past.

Group	Home	Food	Art Forms	Other Facts
The Pueblo				
The Hopi	adobe villages	corn	basket weaving pottery silver work kachina dolls	
The Pima	Permanent home called a sandwich home. It was rectangular. It was built with mud and cactus.	corn, squash, beans	basket making	
The Navajo	Permanent home called a hogan. It was made of wood.	corn, fruit	basket making weaving silver work	sheepherders
The				

Teaching Tips

As you prepare to teach about Native American peoples and their cultures, remember that good information, common sense, thoughtfulness, and sensitivity are your best guides. Always differentiate between the past and the present. Avoid activities that perpetuate stereotypes, such as role-playing or the choosing of "Indian" names. Constantly ask yourself how you are increasing your students' knowledge of these rich cultures and ways of life. And always respect the sacred nature of objects and practices associated with Native American cultures. If you are unsure if an activity is appropriate, the best thing you can do is consult a Native American for advice.

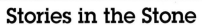

Stories in the Stone

Scattered throughout the Southwest are stone drawings called *petroglyphs*. Even though scientists are not sure what most of the drawings mean, they feel certain that the drawings were one way that native southwesterners communicated.

Draw a few simple characters like the ones shown on this page, and ask students to conclude what each may mean. Then let your students try their hand at creating and deciphering paper petroglyphs. To make his drawing, a child trims a 9" x 12" sheet of tan paper to create a large stone shape. On one side he secretly writes in English a message that a southwestern Native American of long ago may have wished to tell others. On the other side of his cutout, he draws a picture or a series of symbols to convey the message. When the projects are finished, have each child, in turn, show his drawing to his classmates and invite them to decode it. At the conclusion of this activity, students will have a much clearer understanding of why scientists often do not agree on the meanings of Native American petroglyphs!

More About Petroglyphs

Use this picture book to further investigate the stone drawings of the Southwest.

The Same Sun Was in the Sky
Written by Denise Webb & Illustrated by Walter Porter
Northland Publishing Company, 1994
A youngster and his grandfather examine the *petroglyphs* in a southwestern desert and theorize about the ancient people who etched them.

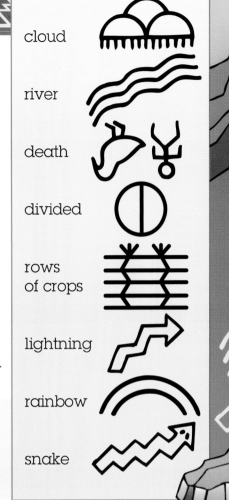

cloud

river

death

divided

rows
of crops

lightning

rainbow

snake

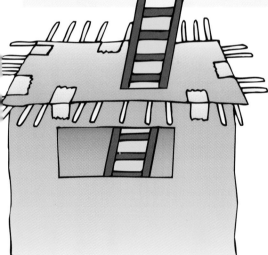

Southwestern Homes

Native southwesterners used materials from their environment to build their homes. Whether a home was permanent or temporary depended on the lifestyle of the builder. Because the Pai and the Apache moved frequently, their homes were easy to build. The Tohono O'odham and Pima peoples, who lived among the desert's saguaro cactus, built homes from mud and cactus ribs. Perhaps the most prevalent structure of the Southwest was the Pueblo home. Each flat-roofed dwelling was constructed from *adobe,* a mixture of clay and sand that covers much of the Southwest.

To construct a Pueblo village in your classroom, have each child create a Pueblo home from a brown paper lunch bag. To do this he cuts away the top six inches of the bag before he opens it. Then he uses scissors, paper scraps, toothpicks, glue or tape, and crayons or markers to craft a roof, a window, an entry hatch, a ladder(s), and other desired details. Arrange the student-made dwellings on a paper-covered table so that you create a village with a central plaza. For added fun, provide modeling clay and invite students to sculpt beehive ovens, native peoples, and other authentic elements for the display.

Did You Know?
- A typical Pueblo adobe home was about 12 feet by 20 feet.
- An adobe home was entered through a hatch in the roof or through a window.
- A family slept on rugs or animal skins. There was no bed.
- There were no tables or chairs.
- Every home had a trough for grinding corn.
- Pueblo houses were generally built by the women.

A Southwestern Affair

People from the world over come to the Southwest to purchase the unrivaled Native American art that is crafted there. One of the largest art-and-craft fairs held each year is the Santa Fe Indian Market. Because art is a fun and educational way to learn about the culture and lifestyles of the first southwesterners, four craft-type projects follow. Boost your youngsters' self-esteem by designating an area of your classroom where students can proudly showcase the Native American art that they create. As an added bonus, the resulting southwestern display is just what you need for an impressive culminating activity (see "It's a Southwestern Celebration!" on page 15).

Pueblo Pottery

Making fine pottery has always been important to the Pueblo. The clay pots made by Pueblo ancestors were used for cooking, serving, and storing food. Today Pueblo artists still hand-form their clay pots. Because Pueblo pottery is prized by collectors from around the world, it is an excellent source of income for many Pueblo Native Americans.

Each student can create her own Pueblo-style pottery using a ball of Crayola Model Magic, a paintbrush, and tempera or acrylic paints. Invite each student to shape her ball of modeling compound into a pot or a small turtle (a shape that many Pueblo children make when they are just beginning to learn about pottery). After the student's pottery piece has dried overnight, have her use the paints and paintbrush to embellish it as desired.

Pam Crane

Stunning Navajo Silver Work

One of the best-known Native American crafts today is the beautiful turquoise-and-silver jewelry made by the Navajo. Surprisingly enough the Navajo only began making the jewelry in the mid-1800s—not all that long ago! Show students photographs (or actual samples) of Navajo jewelry. Explain that the jewelry holds special meaning to the Navajo people because in their culture turquoise represents harmony and beauty.

Students will enjoy making stunning pendants that resemble this Navajo art form. To make a pendant, cover a three-inch tagboard circle with aluminum foil. Use craft glue to attach pieces of turquoise-colored Play-Doh to the foil. When the glue has dried, use a toothpick to carefully etch details into the foil. Securely tape the center of a three-foot length of string or cord to the back of the project. For added appeal crumple small pieces of foil around the string to create shiny silver beads as shown. Tightly tie the string's ends so that the stunning silver work will be easy to slip on and off for wearing. Interested students can also craft bracelets and belts from similar supplies.

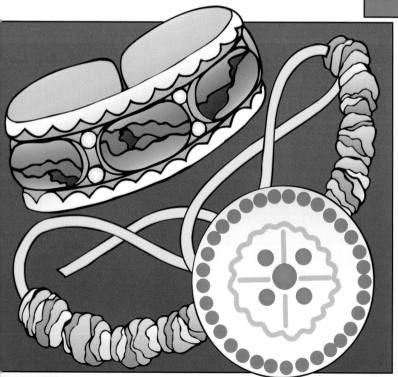

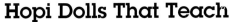

Hopi Dolls That Teach

Perhaps the most distinctive of all Hopi creations are the *kachina dolls.* Each doll is carefully carved from the root of a cottonwood tree and painted to resemble a Hopi spirit or *kachina.* Because there are more than 250 different kachinas in the Hopi culture, Hopi children are often given the dolls as a way to teach them about the spirits. A kachina doll is a very valued possession and is never handled as a toy. Over time the kachina dolls have become very detailed and fanciful, and are now also purchased by non-Hopi collectors from around the world for their artistic beauty.

These colorful, student-created doll booklets are the perfect place to record information about the Hopi. To make his booklet, a student traces a doll-shaped template (like the one shown) onto a cereal-box panel and cuts along the resulting outline. Then he uses colorful paper, glue, markers or crayons, craft feathers, yarn, and other available materials to decorate the cutout to his liking. Assist each student in stapling a stack of blank paper rectangles to the front of the cutout. Next instruct each child to write "Facts About the Hopi" and his name on the top rectangle, then write and illustrate a fact about the Hopi Indians on each remaining rectangle. Encourage students to use their completed booklets to *teach* their family and friends about the Hopi.

Apache Baskets

Traditionally the Apache were hunters and gatherers who frequently moved from place to place in search of food. Breakable clay pots were impractical for this lifestyle, so the Apache used yucca, beargrass, and other plants to weave light baskets in which to store and carry food and water. Today the Apache make beautiful baskets for use in ceremonies and to sell to collectors. The following basket-weaving project is sure to please your students. For the best results, complete Steps 1 and 2 for each student in advance.

Lightweight Basket

Materials needed for one basket:

9-ounce clear plastic cup	clear tape
natural twine: four 1-foot lengths	scissors
raffia: two or more different colors	hole puncher
masking or colored electric tape	ruler

Directions:

1. In the cup make an odd number of vertical cuts that are about one inch apart and stop at the base.
2. Punch two holes in the cup rim opposite each other.
3. To prevent raveling, tape each end of each twine length with the masking tape.
4. Holding the center portion of one twine length taut, slide the twine to the base of the container through two opposite slits.
5. Repeat Step 4 two more times, varying the placement of each twine length.
6. Tie and knot one end of a length of raffia around one plastic strip—making sure the raffia is pushed to the base of the cup and the knot is to the inside.
7. Weave the entire length of raffia in and out of the plastic strips, making sure the exposed end is inside the cup.
8. Varying the color of the raffia used as desired, repeat Steps 6 and 7—starting where the last length of raffia ended—until the cup is covered.
9. Use the clear tape to secure any loose ends of raffia inside the cup.
10. To make a basket handle, thread and tie each end of the remaining twine length through a different hole in the cup rim.

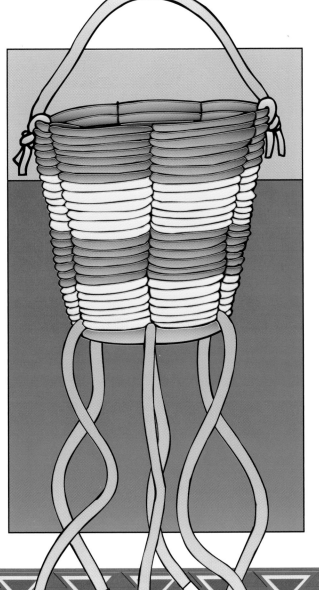

A Taste of the Southwest

One of the main crops of the first Native Americans living in the Southwest was corn. In time other crops like pumpkins, squash, and beans were cultivated. Add to the flavor of your southwestern study by preparing a corn dish. It could be as simple as popping corn for the class or baking corn muffins. If you're a bit more adventurous, try one of the following recipes.

Navajo Faux Fry Bread
(makes about 25 small servings)

Ingredients:
2 cups self-rising cornmeal
1 1/2 cups buttermilk
2 eggs
2 tablespoons sugar

Directions:
Mix the ingredients together. Using an electric fry pan or a skillet and a hot plate, prepare spoonfuls of the batter as you would pancakes.

Pueblo Corn Pudding
(makes about 25 small servings)

Ingredients:
3 cups milk
1/2 cup molasses or
    dark corn syrup
1/3 cup cornmeal
2 eggs, slightly beaten

2 tablespoons melted butter
1 1/2 tsp. pumpkin pie spice
1/8 tsp. salt

Directions:
In a large saucepan, stir together the milk and molasses. Cook over medium heat until hot—but not boiling. Slowly stir in the cornmeal. Continue cooking and stirring. When the mixture thickens, remove it from the heat, and stir in the eggs and butter. Next add the pumpkin pie spice and the salt. Stir until well blended. Spray the bottom and sides of a square baking pan with nonstick cooking spray, and pour the mixture into the pan. Bake at 325° for about 1 hour and 15 minutes. Let the pudding cool; then cut it into squares to serve. Top each serving with a dab of whipped cream if desired.

A Southwestern Trickster

Coyote is a trickster celebrated in folklore the world over. But he is arguably the most famous in the American Southwest. Coyote is both a trickster and a wise teacher. He survives against impossible odds; however, no matter how tricky he is, he is usually the brunt of his own joke or trick. Read aloud a sampling of Coyote trickster tales from the Southwest. Two possible selections are reviewed on pages 16 and 17. Another story worth considering is *Coyote and the Magic Words* written by Phyllis Root and illustrated by Sandra Speidel (Lothrop, Lee & Shepard Books; 1993). Then invite each child to write and illustrate an original story featuring this southwestern trickster. Mount each child's work on colorful paper, and exhibit it on a bulletin board titled "Coyote Tales."

Outstanding Teacher Resources

Desert Dwellers: Native People of the American Southwest
Written & Photographed by Scott S. Warren
Chronicle Books, 1997

Pueblo Indian
Written by Steven Cory & Illustrated by Richard Erickson
Lerner Publications Company, 1996

The Navajos: People of the Southwest
Written by Nancy Bonvillain & Includes Photographs
The Millbrook Press, Inc.; 1995

Keeping the Culture Alive

It is important that students understand that Native American culture is an important part of our country's past *and* its future. Use the following literature selections to introduce students to some present-day Native American children who are proudly carrying on the heritage of their southwestern ancestors. Students will enjoy discovering the similarities and the differences between their lives and the lives of the children they learn about.

books reviewed by Deborah Zink Roffino

Dancing Rainbows: A Pueblo Boy's Story
Written & Photographed by Evelyn Clarke Mott
Cobblehill Books, 1996

A young Tewa boy and his grandfather invite readers to join them as they prepare for their tribe's annual Feast Day celebration. Vivid photographs capture the preparations and provide a detailed look at colorful costumes and dances that are an important part of this traditional event.

Earth Daughter: Alicia of Ácoma Pueblo
Written & Photographed by George Ancona
Simon & Schuster Books For Young Readers, 1995

Family and culture are celebrated in this inviting look at a Pueblo people and their time-honored art of pottery making. Full-color close-ups bring the pottery-making process to life—from searching for just the right clay to selling the completed pieces at a festive Pueblo craft fair.

Pueblo Boy: Growing Up in Two Worlds
Written & Photographed by Marcia Keegan
Puffin Books, 1991

This slim paperback is a beautifully executed photo-essay of the day-to-day life of Timmy Roybal, a ten-year-old Native American growing up at the San Ildefonso Pueblo in New Mexico.

Apache Rodeo
Written by Diane Hoyt-Goldsmith
Photographed by Lawrence Migdale
Holiday House, Inc.; 1995

Ten-year-old Felecita provides the narration for this superbly photographed visit to the Fort Apache Reservation in Whiteriver, Arizona. Her enthusiasm for traditional Apache events like the annual rodeo is contagious. And her descriptions of everyday events and activities will lead students to see the similarities between their lives and life on the reservation.

My Navajo Sister
Written & Illustrated by Eleanor Schick
Simon & Schuster Books For Young Readers, 1996

A young girl fondly remembers a summer spent living on a ranch near a Navajo reservation. Wispy pastels capture the memories, Navajo culture, and Arizona landscape.

A Rainbow at Night: The World in Words and Pictures by Navajo Children
Written by Bruce Hucko
Chronicle Books, 1996

Through this lively collection of paintings and drawings, youngsters will learn about special traditions of Navajo life and the kinship that all children—regardless of their backgrounds—share. Each piece of artwork is accompanied by a photo of and a quote from the artist, a brief paragraph of explanation and/or insight, and a suggested follow-up activity from the children's "art coach."

It's a Southwestern Celebration!

Conclude your study of southwestern Native Americans with a festival of learning! Encourage students to invite their families to this special celebration. The guests of honor can stroll through the classroom area where student projects are on display (see "A Southwestern Affair" on page 12), check out the student-created Pueblo village (see "Southwestern Homes" on page 11), and read the Coyote tales on exhibit (see "A Southwestern Trickster" on page 14). Plan for students to serve their guests a southwestern snack that includes a sample of fry bread or corn pudding (recipes on page 14). Then invite interested youngsters to share what they have learned about Native Americans of the Southwest and to field questions from their visitors on the topic. Conclude the festivities with an oral reading of one or more student-selected Native American picture books: fiction, nonfiction, or both!

Folklore From The American Southwest

Provide additional insight into the customs and cultures of the Native Americans of the Southwest with this sampling of entertaining stories.

books reviewed by Deborah Zink Roffino

Ahaiyute and Cloud Eater
Written by Vladimir Hulpach & Illustrated by Marek Zawadzki
Harcourt Brace & Company, 1996

Tense drama, ancient wisdom, and lustrous paintings blend to create a memorable tale of a young Zuni brave. Anxious to earn recognition as a warrior, the boy accepts a challenge to conquer a long-feared cloud-eating beast. The interaction between the boy and the animal that guides him clearly captures the core of Native American folklore.

The Turkey Girl: A Zuni Cinderella Story
Retold by Penny Pollock & Illustrated by Ed Young
Little, Brown And Company; 1996

Wistful, smoky pastels cast a mournful glow across the pages of this age-old Zuni tale that—until its ending—bears a strong resemblance to its European counterpart. A young orphan girl, who lovingly tends turkeys for a living, longs to attend a festival dance. Thanks to her faithful flock, she goes to the dance with the promise to return before the sun has set. Caught up in the music and the moment, the young maiden makes an irreversible choice that forever saddens her heart.

Coyote: A Trickster Tale From the American Southwest
Told & Illustrated by Gerald McDermott
Harcourt Brace & Company, 1994

Coyote is misbehaving again, and this time it's his own vanity that gets him into a heap of trouble. Insistent on becoming the greatest coyote in the world, he convinces a flock of crows to teach him how to sing, dance, and fly. But the crows soon tire of Coyote's never ending boasting and bragging, and decide to teach the trickster a lifelong lesson!

The Flute Player: An Apache Folktale
Retold & Illustrated by Michael Lacapa
Northland Publishing Company, 1996

Brush strokes of bold watercolor brighten the pages of this tender love story. When the sounds of a young brave's flute echo through the red-walled canyon, only a maiden knows that the melody is not the wind, but a song for her. One day the flute player is called away, but his maiden knows only that the music has stopped. When the brave returns, he is devastated to discover that his maiden has died from a broken heart. Forever after, throughout the steep canyon, his melancholy flute echoes—often mistaken for the wind.

Antelope Woman: An Apache Folktale
Retold & Illustrated by Michael Lacapa
Northland Publishing Company, 1995

Apache tradition teaches many things: respect for the earth, thankfulness for great and small things, an appreciation of family. Native American artist and storyteller Lacapa inscribes these values into this tale of a young girl who becomes an antelope to follow her one true love. Bright, bold colors coupled with the jagged geometrics of Apache art create a stunning tribute to a people who are totally in tune with the earth.

How the Stars Fell Into the Sky: A Navajo Legend
Written by Jerrie Oughton & Illustrated by Lisa Desimini
Houghton Mifflin Company, 1992

In this Navajo folktale, hardworking First Woman devises a remarkable plan to display all of the laws necessary for mankind to live in peace on earth. Using the whole night sky as her canvas, she takes her precious jewels and lovingly nestles them in the sky, carefully and patiently spelling out the laws for all to see. Realizing the time involved in such an important job, First Woman readily accepts Coyote's offer to help. But Coyote becomes impatient with the tedious task and impulsively flings her twinkling treasures into the night sky.

The Magic of Spider Woman
Written by Lois Duncan & Illustrated by Shonto Begay
Scholastic Inc., 1996

Teaching lessons of love, creativity, and moderation, this legend is based on oral traditions of the Navajo. The Spider Woman instructs Wandering Girl in the skill of weaving, but warns her that sitting at the loom for too long will create imbalance in her life and bring about unfavorable consequences. Frothy paintings full of mystery and rich tones reveal details of Navajo land, dwellings, clothing, and blankets.

Arrow to the Sun: A Pueblo Indian Tale
Adapted & Illustrated by Gerald McDermott
Puffin Books, 1974

In this Caldecott Medal book, McDermott offers a traditional Pueblo Indian tale in celebration of the life-sustaining power of the Sun. Dancing geometric images in sizzling desert colors tell of a young boy in search of his father, the Sun. Crisp, sparse text encourages imaginative reading.

Eagle Boy: A Traditional Navajo Legend
Retold by Gerald Hausman & Illustrated by Cara and Barry Moser
HarperCollins Children's Books, 1996

Misty pastels create a dreamy background for this Navajo legend that honors the first medicine man. A curious little boy with a special affinity for eagles is lifted into the sky to learn the healing ways of the sacred birds. When he returns home, he has a new name and a knowledge that will enable him to become a great medicine man.

Dragonfly's Tale
Retold & Illustrated by Kristina Rodanas
Clarion Books, 1992

The age-old theme of gratitude hovers above this ancient Zuni tale of the Ashiwi people like the nimble fluttering of a dragonfly. The Corn Maidens have blessed their favored children with friendly rains, fertile earth, and abundant harvest. But the Ashiwi take their bounty for granted and squander it away. Aided by a magic cornstalk insect, two children toil to restore the precious gifts.

Crow and Hawk: A Traditional Pueblo Indian Story
Retold by Michael Rosen & Illustrated by John Clementson
Harcourt Brace & Company, 1995

This traditional Pueblo Indian story tells of two birds that vie for the ownership of a nest full of eggs. Crow lays the eggs, then leaves her nest unattended. Hawk spots the unattended nest, takes pity on the eggs, and raises the chicks as if they were her own. It's a flap that must be mediated by Eagle, the King of the Birds. Vivid cut-paper designs energize the pages as Eagle shares his wisdom.

The Girl Who Loved Coyotes: Stories of the Southwest
Written by Nancy Wood & Illustrated by Diana Bryer
Morrow Junior Books, 1995

Each of the 12 original stories in this delightful collection revolves around the coyote, a figure of legend among primitive peoples the world over. Decorated with brilliant, framed paintings, the stories resonate with the enduring spirit of the Southwest and remind listeners of the need for justice, fair treatment of animals, and preservation of our natural environment.

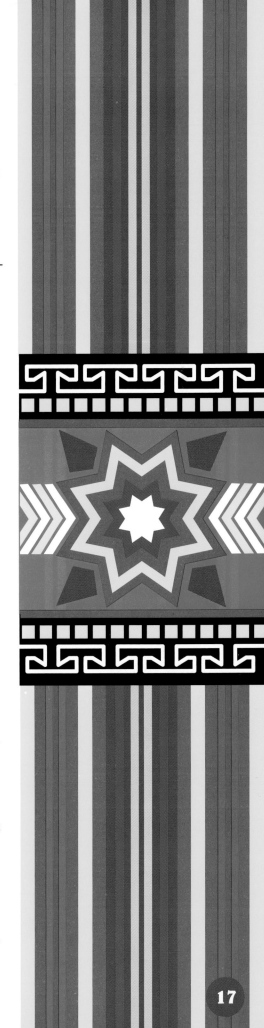

Native Americans of the Plains

Hundreds of years ago buffalo roamed freely on the Plains of North America where untold numbers of Native Americans lived and hunted. Use these activities to introduce students to the native people of the Plains, their customs of the past, and traditions that carry on today.

by Vicki Mockaitis Dabrowka—Gr. 2, Concord Hill School, Chevy Chase, MD

Pinpointing the Plains

The Plains of North America stretch from the Mississippi River to the Rocky Mountains and from Canada's Saskatchewan River to central Texas. It is a vast region of flat prairies and gently rolling hills. As you show students this area on a U.S. map, explain that the native people who lived here long ago endured extremely cold winters, intense summer heat, droughts, sudden dust storms, and plenty more. Invite students to contemplate how they coped with these conditions. Then have each child complete the mapping activity on page 22.

Two Distinct Regions

Long ago the wide-reaching plains were home to more than 30 Native American nations. While each had its own unique culture, belief system, and language, the environment determined the homes and food supply of the people. Use a Venn diagram to reveal the two distinct regions of the Plains and to explore the similarities and differences among the native people who lived there. Draw and label a diagram that resembles the one shown. In each section, list the provided information and discuss it with the class. Next have each child copy the diagram onto a large sheet of drawing paper and add desired artwork. Suggest that students keep these projects handy so they can continue to add facts throughout their study.

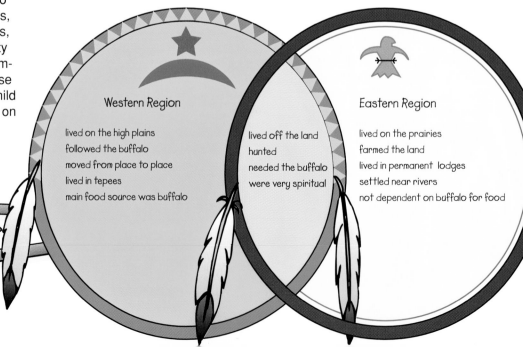

Western Region
- lived on the high plains
- followed the buffalo
- moved from place to place
- lived in tepees
- main food source was buffalo

- lived off the land
- hunted
- needed the buffalo
- were very spiritual

Eastern Region
- lived on the prairies
- farmed the land
- lived in permanent lodges
- settled near rivers
- not dependent on buffalo for food

High Plains and Prairies

Use this informative chant to reinforce the way of life on the western high plains and eastern prairies of the North American Plains. For added fun, engage students in clapping a rhythmic background beat during the chant.

High Plains and Prairies

The people of the high plains long ago
Hunted and followed the buffalo,
Moving their tepees and arrows.
A need for food kept them on the go.

Off to the east, where the prairies were,
Planting and hunting did occur.
Big earth lodges did not stir.
These people stayed right where they were.

Homes on the Plains

Native Americans of long ago used materials from their environment to build homes that best suited their needs. Enlist your youngsters' help in converting a classroom table into a representation of the Plains. To do this, have each child make one of the Native American homes described below. Display the completed projects on a large classroom table covered with brown paper—tepees to the west, earth lodges to the east. Invite students to add grass, leaves, buffalo fashioned from construction paper, and other elements of the environment to the display.

Tepee

The tepee, which was both permanent and mobile, was a practical dwelling for the hunters of the western Plains. To erect a tepee, a framework of long, straight poles (tied together near the top) was set upright and covered with buffalo hides sewn together and decorated with traditional painted designs.

To make a replica of a tepee, a student uses crayons or markers to decorate a tan construction paper copy of the pattern on page 23. Then she cuts out the pattern and glues the tab to the straight edge so that a cone shape results. When the glue is dry, she makes an entrance flap by cutting a slit in the bottom edge of the tepee and folding back the paper. Then she glues a few toothpicks in the small hole at the top.

Earth Lodge

The most common dwelling to the east was the earth lodge—a large, circular structure with a square smoke hole at the top and a covered porchlike structure, or *vestibule,* at the entrance of the lodge. Each permanent home housed 30 to 40 people. A lodge was built by erecting a large wooden framework and then covering it with layers of branches, grass, and earth.

To make a replica of an earth lodge, precut a small square hole in the bottom of a Chinet bowl. A student inverts the prepared bowl, trims away the outer rim, and cuts an opening for the vestibule. Keeping the bowl inverted, he sponge-paints it using brown tempera paint that contains a bit of glue. Next he presses dried grass, torn bits of paper, or small pieces of unraveled twine atop the painted surface. Then he adds another layer of paint. Last he rolls a brown paper rectangle into a cylinder, inserts it into the opening of the lodge to create a vestibule, and uses glue or tape as needed to secure it in place.

Signs of Communication

The Plains of North America were home to numerous groups of Native Americans, which meant that many different languages were spoken there. As a result, the people of the Plains often used sign language to communicate. Today sign language is still a very important part of Native American culture and tradition, even though spoken language is more often used. Set aside time for students to communicate using traditional Native American sign language. To do this, distribute student copies of the communication card on page 23, pair the youngsters, and challenge partners to silently communicate with each other using the provided gestures. Then bring the class together to discuss the challenges of this type of communication. Later make available *Native American Sign Language* by Madeline Olsen (Troll Associates, Inc.; 1998). This slim paperback offers more than 100 traditional signs for students to learn and use.

A Taste of the Plains

Buffalo was hunted and eaten by all native people of the Plains. It was the main food source on the western Plains, where the land was unsuitable for farming. Wild berries and roots were harvested across the Plains. To the east where the land was fertile, crops of corn, squash, beans, and pumpkins also provided nourishment. Native Americans dried their food to preserve it for year-round eating. For a taste of the Plains of long ago, provide samples of jerky, dried berries, pumpkin seeds, and popcorn for students to eat.

As students enjoy a taste of the Plains, read aloud *Heetunka's Harvest: A Tale of the Plains Indians* by Jennifer Berry Jones (Roberts Rinehart Publishers, 1998). In this beautifully illustrated retelling of a Sioux legend, a greedy woman learns a hard lesson about selfishness.

The Sky Dog

When the horse appeared on the Plains of North America in the 1500s, the lives of the people living there greatly improved. Hunters no longer traveled on foot. Instead they chased down buffalo herds on horseback. More captured buffalo resulted in more food, clothing, and other supplies (see "Buffalo Fact Box" on this page). The horse, respectfully called Sky Dog, Holy Dog, Sacred Dog, and many other names by Native Americans, was believed to be a sacred gift from the Great Spirit.

To further inform students of the importance of the horse, read aloud *The Gift of the Sacred Dog* by Paul Goble (Aladdin Paperbacks, 1984). Then give each child a portion of modeling clay from which to mold a horse shape. While students work, consider reading aloud another enchanting tale from the Plains, such as *The Mud Pony* retold by Caron Lee Cohen (Scholastic Inc., 1992). Invite students to display their clay creations on your tabletop reproduction of the Plains (see "Homes on the Plains" on page 19).

Buffalo Fact Box
No part of a buffalo was wasted!

meat	=	food
bones	=	tools, weapons, pipes
intestines	=	cord
hooves	=	jewelry, glue, utensils
horns	=	cups, spoons
hides	=	clothing, moccasins, homes
hair	=	rope, padding

The Vision Quest

One tradition among the people of the Plains was for a boy coming of age to learn of his calling in life during a *vision quest*. At this time, he set out alone, without food or water, for a specific location. Here he prayed that his future be revealed. Tomie dePaola's book *The Legend of the Indian Paintbrush* (PaperStar, 1996) artfully describes this quest through its main character, Little Gopher. Read this story aloud and then challenge students to recall how and why Little Gopher was encouraged to celebrate his unique talents. Next invite students to talk about their special talents or interests. For a thought-provoking follow-up, have each child tear from a brown paper grocery bag a shape that resembles an animal hide. Then ask him to paint on this paper a picture that reflects a special talent or interest. When the paintings are dry, have each child use a marker to sign the bottom of his work. Then display the projects on a bulletin board titled "Painting Our Futures."

The Powwow

The powwow is the oldest North American celebration. Today it continues to be an important expression of togetherness among not only those whose ancestors lived off the Plains, but for all Native Americans. Each year in cities and towns across the United States and Canada, Native Americans from far and near gather to celebrate their culture and share it with non-Native American visitors. Read aloud chosen titles from "Powwow Reading." Next gather students together and ask each child to share one thing he learned about the Native Americans of the Plains. Then, in the tradition of a modern-day powwow giveaway, scatter wrapped candy around the classroom and invite students to collect the candy for eating!

A Reminder About Native American Studies

As you teach about Native American people and their cultures, remember that good information, common sense, thoughtfulness, and sensitivity are your best guides. Always differentiate between the past and the present. Avoid activities that perpetuate stereotypes, such as role-playing or the choosing of "Indian" names. Constantly ask yourself how you are increasing your students' knowledge of these rich cultures and ways of life. And always respect the sacred nature of objects and practices associated with Native American cultures. If you are unsure whether an activity is appropriate, the best thing you can do is consult a Native American for advice.

Powwow Reading

Celebrating the Powwow
Written by Bobbie Kalman
Includes photographs
Crabtree Publishing Company, 1997

Rainy's Powwow
Written by Linda Theresa Raczek
Illustrated by Gary Bennett
Rising Moon, 1999

Powwow
Written & photographed by
    George Ancona
Harcourt Brace Jovanovich,
    Publishers; 1993

Drumbeat...Heartbeat:
A Celebration of the Powwow
Written & photographed by
    Susan Braine
Lerner Publications Company, 1995

Name

A Home on the Plains

Color the map.
First color where the Native Americans of the Plains once lived.
Then color the rest of the map. Use the map key.

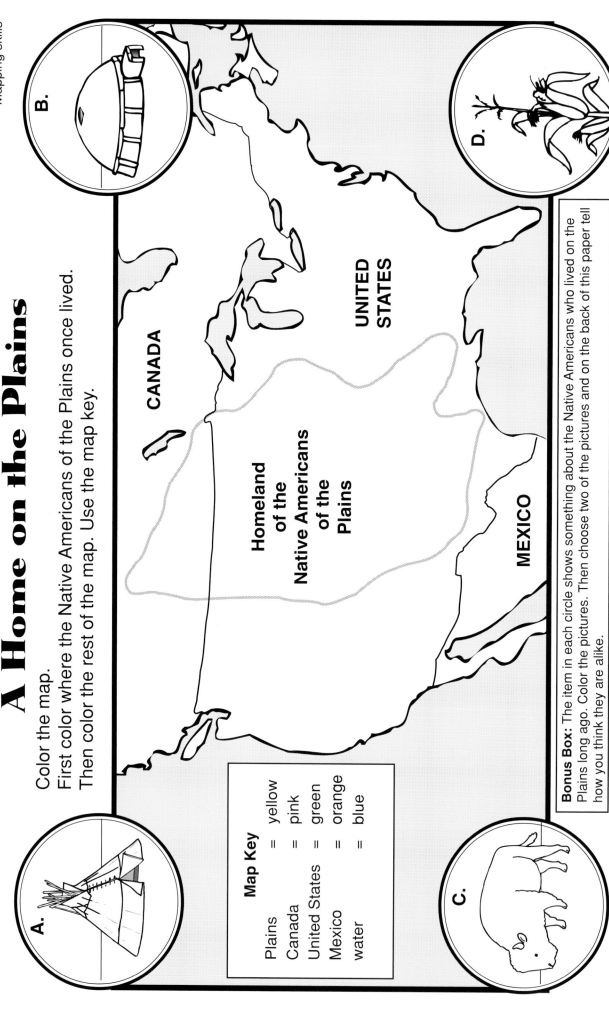

CANADA

UNITED
STATES

Homeland
of the
Native Americans
of the
Plains

MEXICO

Map Key

Plains	=	yellow
Canada	=	pink
United States	=	green
Mexico	=	orange
water	=	blue

A.

B.

C.

D.

Bonus Box: The item in each circle shows something about the Native Americans who lived on the Plains long ago. Color the pictures. Then choose two of the pictures and on the back of this paper tell how you think they are alike.

©The Education Center, Inc. • *Native Americans* • Primary • TEC3236

Note to the teacher: Use with "Pinpointing the Plains" on page 18.

Tab

Use card with "Signs of Communication" on page 20.

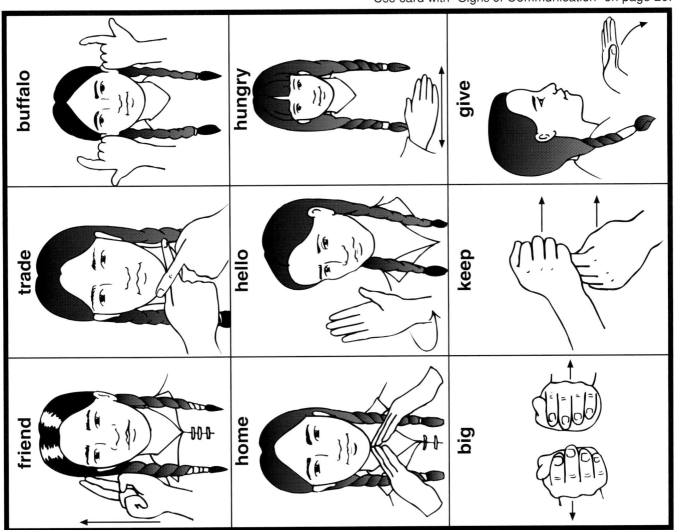

buffalo	hungry	give
trade	hello	keep
friend	home	big

Natives of the Eastern Woodlands

Long before Columbus arrived in America, there were countless groups of native peoples living off the land. The heavily wooded area along the East Coast was home to many of these people. Use the following activities and literature suggestions to help students gain a better understanding of—and an appreciation for—the rich cultures of our first Americans.

ideas contributed by Geraldine Nemirow
books reviewed by Deborah Zink Roffino

The Eastern Woodlands

The dense forests that stretched along the Atlantic coast—south from Canada to Florida and as far west as the Mississippi River—became known as the Eastern Woodlands. Locate this large region on a map of the United States. Assist students in finding mountain ranges, lakes, and rivers within the area. Talk with your students about the Eastern Woodlands. Have them describe what they think this land would have been like long ago. Ask students to explain how the land changed. Find out if they know why these changes occurred. *(Note: Some references separate the Eastern Woodlands into two regions—the Northeast Woodlands, or Great Forest, and the Southeast. We have chosen to address the Eastern Woodlands as one large region.)*

Helpful Information

The Native Americans who lived in the Eastern Woodlands consisted of four main tribal groups. One group embodied numerous tribes of Algonquin Indians. These peoples lived to the northeast, as did the peoples of the Iroquois Nation—another of the four main groups. The Creek Confederacy (or Muskogee Indian Nation) lived to the southeast, and the fourth group of Native Americans lived around the Great Lakes. This unit explores the Eastern Woodlands and investigates how Native Americans living within this large area adapted their lifestyles to their environments.

Eastern Woodlands

Teaching Tips

As you prepare to teach about Native American peoples and their cultures, remember that good information, common sense, thoughtfulness, and sensitivity are your best guides. Avoid activities that perpetuate stereotypes such as role-playing or the choosing of "Indian" names. Constantly ask yourself how you are increasing your students' knowledge of these rich cultures and ways of life. And always respect the sacred nature of objects and practices associated with the Native American cultures. If you are unsure if an activity is appropriate, the best thing you can do is contact a Native American person for advice.

No Pockets!

Woodland Indians dressed in clothing made from animal skins. The type of day-to-day clothing worn depended on the outside temperature. In warm temperatures, less clothing was worn. In cool temperatures, clothing was added. Decorated clothing was worn for special occasions.

This quick math activity is a fun way to inform students that long ago Native American clothing had no pockets. Divide students into small groups and ask each group to determine how many pockets are being worn in the group. With the students' assistance, tally the group totals, and add to this sum the number of pockets you're wearing. If desired, add to this total any coat and/or sweater pockets that have not been included. Your classroom pocket total should be quite impressive! Ask students how they use pockets and why they do or do not like them. Then reveal that there were no pockets in the clothing worn by Native Americans. Invite students to deduce possible reasons for this and ponder how small items such as food and/or tools were carried. Guide students to conclude that Native Americans carried these items in small pouches that hung from their waists or around their shoulders.

Booklet of Woodland Homes

Native Americans of long ago built their homes using materials from their environment. Whether a home was permanent or temporary depended upon the lifestyle of the Eastern people and the season of the year. Because the Eastern Woodlands area extended so far north and south, there was a large variance of temperature and terrain within the region. This resulted in several different styles of dwellings. Use the booklet project on page 30 to introduce students to four different types of homes that were built in the Woodlands region.

Duplicate a class supply of page 30 on white construction paper. As a class, read about each dwelling. Help students locate on their maps the general area where each type of house was built. As students color the picture of the dwelling, tell them a little bit more about it by reading aloud the information from the box below. When all four dwellings have been discussed and colored, each student cuts on the dotted lines. Then he stacks the booklet cover and pages, and staples them to the pattern.

- The Algonquins used bark from birch, chestnut, oak, or elm trees to cover their homes. When the Algonquins were away from their village on a hunt, they put up cone-shaped homes made of wooden poles and bark.

- Several family groups shared the Iroquois longhouse. Inside the house each family had an open fire in the center of its assigned area. In an Iroquois village there would be many longhouses. Most villages had high fences built around them for protection.

- More than one family lived in the Cherokee house. In the winter, mats made from branches, cattails, and cornhusks were added to the outside walls for protection from the weather. A Cherokee village was surrounded by a high fence. A large, round Council House stood in the middle of the village, and the chief's dwelling was nearby.

- The Choctaw type of housing reflects the semitropical nature of the Southern Woodlands. The Seminole also lived in the southeastern region. Their summer shelter was a wooden platform raised off the ground. It had a roof similar to the Choctaw home, but it had no walls!

Eating Off the Land

The availability of food depended on the season, but since the woodlands teemed with wildlife, there was always large and small game to be hunted. The lakes and rivers were full of fish, and those people who lived near a bay had lobsters, clams, and oysters. In the spring, summer, and fall, there were wild fruits, berries, and nuts, along with an abundance of corn, beans, squash, and other crops. When corn was in season, the woodland peoples cooked a variety of corn dishes including corn soup and cornbread. They popped corn too!

Add to the flavor of your Native American study by preparing a desired corn dish. It could be as simple as popping corn for the class or baking cornbread. If you're a bit more adventurous, try one of the following recipes:

Hominy
(Makes about 25 small servings)

Ingredients:
2 15-oz. cans hominy
1 15-oz. can pinto beans
1 cup cubed ham
pepper to taste

Directions:
Combine ingredients. Heat and serve.

Oneida Corn Soup
(Makes about 25 small servings)

Ingredients:
1 cup fresh spinach, torn
1 15-oz. can whole-kernel corn
½ cup cooked beef cut into small pieces
½ cup long grain rice
1 quart water
1 tsp. salt
pepper to taste

Directions:
Combine ingredients in a medium pot. Simmer until rice is cooked (25–30 minutes).

Building With Birch

Many natives of the Eastern Woodlands made houses, canoes, and many different types of utensils and containers using birch bark. The Native American women fashioned the utensils and containers. It took lots of patience and skill to punch holes in the bark with bone awls, then stitch the seams together with roots, fibers, or animal tendons. Some items made from birch bark were strengthened with sapling branches or roots, waterproofed with an application of tree gum, and painted with symbols.

This paper-bowl art project helps students understand some of the steps that had to be taken to make a basic bowl. To make this bowl, use a template to trace two large circles of equal size on white or tan bulletin-board paper. To give the paper the appearance of birch bark, lay it atop corrugated cardboard and color the paper using the side of a crayon. Cut out both circles and glue the cutouts back-to-back. Carefully crumple the project; then flatten it and allow it to dry. Cut four pie-wedge shapes in the circle and hole-punch three holes along each cut edge as shown. Lace each pie-wedge shape closed by threading a length of yarn through the six holes and tying the yarn ends.

Spoken Stories

Long ago most Native Americans passed down tribal stories and poetry from one generation to another by word of mouth. Help students develop an appreciation for this oral tradition by asking each child to recall a family story she has been told, a story she has recently read, or a poem that she has memorized. Then pair students and have each child tell her story or poem to her partner. After each partner has taken her turn, gather the youngsters in a large group and invite them to pass on the stories and poems they've just heard. Conclude the storytelling session by asking students to share what they learned from their storytelling experiences.

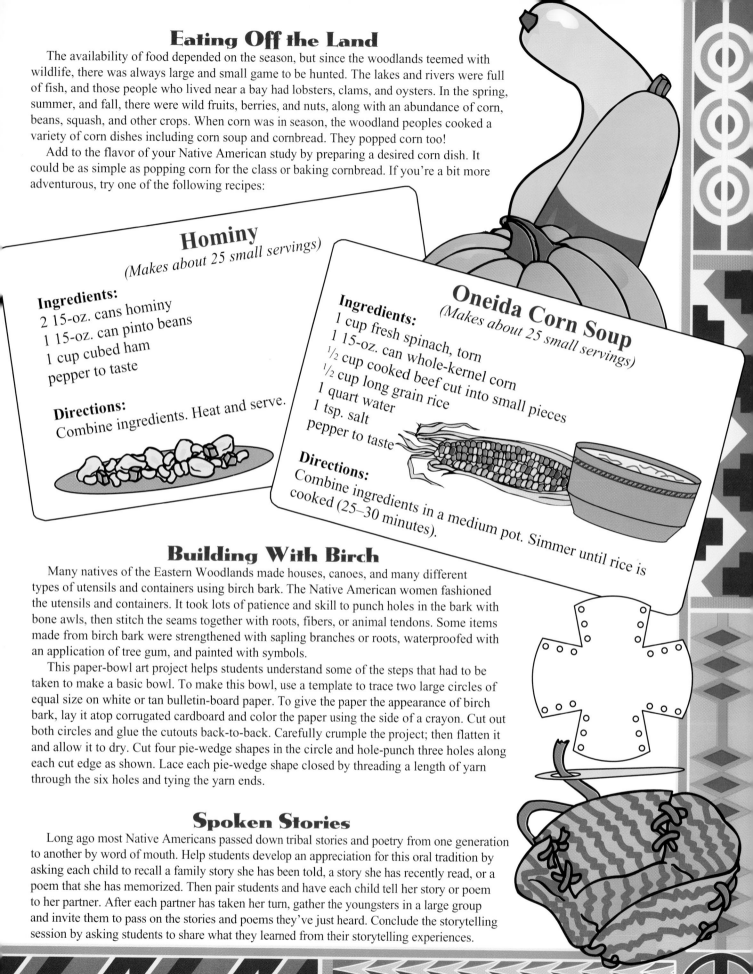

Myths, Legends, and Stories

There are numerous Native American stories written and illustrated for sharing with young children. Some offer explanations for things that occur in nature. Others tell of Native American heroes and heroines. Many teach lessons. The following books are retellings of stories that originated in the Eastern Woodlands. After reading a selection aloud, lead a discussion about the traits of each main character. Then invite students to summarize the story and tell what they learned from the entertaining tale.

Gluskabe and the Four Wishes

Retold by Joseph Bruchac
Illustrated by Christine Nyburg Shrader
Cobblehill Books, 1995

The story of Gluskabe and the four wishes is a traditional story told in various ways among the Wabanaki peoples of New England. In this retelling four Abenaki men set out on a treacherous journey to a far-off island to ask Gluskabe—helper of the Great Spirit—to grant each of them a wish. Gluskabe listens to the four wishes and gives each man a pouch that is not to be opened until the man reaches his home. Powerful paintings grace the pages of this Native American tale that carries an important lesson.

The Story of the Milky Way: A Cherokee Tale

Retold by Joseph Bruchac and Gayle Ross
Illustrated by Virginia A. Stroud
Dial Books For Young Readers, 1995

How did the Milky Way come to be? This story tells how the Cherokee people explained this sparkling, dusty pathway of stars. A lyrical text and exquisite paintings accentuate this superlative story's timeless message: great things can be accomplished when a community works together.

Old Meshikee and the Little Crabs

Retold by Michael Spooner and Lolita Taylor
Illustrated by John Hart
Henry Holt And Company, Inc.; 1996

In this playful retelling of a traditional Ojibwe folktale, a village of crabs devises an outrageous plan to restore peace and quiet to their lakeshore community. But the clever crabs quickly discover that dealing with noisy Old Meshikee—a turtle who is very old and very wise—is much more difficult than they'd anticipated. Perhaps they'll outsmart Old Meshikee another day!

The Great Ball Game: A Muskogee Story

Retold by Joseph Bruchac
Illustrated by Susan L. Roth
Dial Books For Young Readers, 1994

This amusing folktale from the Muskogee, or Creek, Indian Nation, describes a legendary ball game played between the Birds and the Animals in an effort to settle a disagreement. The fast-paced game and brilliant collage artwork offer satisfying proof that size and skill need not be relative. Readers also learn why the Birds fly south in the winter!

More Stories From the Woodlands

How Turtle's Back Was Cracked: A Traditional Cherokee Tale
Retold by Gayle Ross & Illustrated by Murv Jacob
Dial Books For Young Readers, 1995

How Thunder and Lightning Came to Be: A Choctaw Legend
Retold by Beatrice Orcutt Harrell & Illustrated by Susan L. Roth
Dial Books For Young Readers, 1995

The First Strawberries: A Cherokee Story
Retold by Joseph Bruchac & Illustrated by Anna Vojtech
Dial Books For Young Readers, 1993

Sootface: An Ojibwa Cinderella Story
Retold by Robert D. San Souci & Illustrated by Daniel San Souci
Bantam Doubleday Dell Books For Young Readers, 1994

Learning About Wampum

Wampum beads held social, political, and religious significance to the natives of the Northeast Woodlands. It was only after the settlers arrived that wampum began to be used as money in trade. Dark wampum beads—which ranged from purple or blue to black—had about twice the value of white wampum beads. Both kinds of wampum were made from pieces of shell. To make a wampum bead, a hole was bored in both ends of a shell piece. When the holes met, a stone was used to smooth the shell down to a small bead about one-quarter inch wide and one-half inch thick. Wampum beads were strung in strands to make necklaces, belts, and sashes. Oftentimes the beads were strung so that they conveyed messages or recorded important events.

At a center place a container of dried navy beans and a container of dried black beans along with several shoebox lids and a picture of a wampum belt. Working inside a box lid, a student uses the colored beans to fashion a design for a wampum belt that conveys a message or records an important event. No doubt after working with these small beans, your youngsters will have a greater appreciation of the patience and skill that it takes to make and work with wampum!

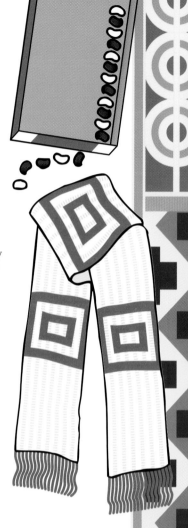

Teaching the Children

Early Native American children learned by listening to their parents and other grown-ups, and by watching and copying the way that things were done. They learned the history, arts, and customs of their people; how to take care of themselves; and how to be at home in the woodlands. As a class, brainstorm the kinds of things that children of the woodlands needed to know. For example, how would a child know which plants were poisonous? When your list is complete, have students suggest how the children might have learned each item listed. Then invite students to talk about the things that they can learn today from their parents and other adults.

Work and Play

There was always plenty of work for the adults. Children did their share of work too. They quickly learned how to swim, how to paddle and steer a canoe, and how to hunt and gather food. Boys learned how to strip the bark off the white birch tree and sew it over the frame of a canoe. Girls learned how to plant crops, prepare food, and make twine from plant fibers. But even in these busy times, Native Americans had time for recreation. Games of chance and skill were very popular. The following games that were played by Eastern Woodland natives can easily be played in the classroom.

Deer Buttons
Number of players: two
Materials needed: eight white buttons with one side on each painted black, box lid, 50 beans in a pot
To play: In turn each player shakes the buttons in his hands and drops them in the box lid. If six white or six black buttons are showing, the player takes two beans from the pot. If seven of the same-color buttons are showing, the player takes four beans from the pot. If all the buttons are the same color, the player takes 20 beans from the pot. Once all the beans are taken from the pot, a player takes beans from his opponent. The game is over when one player has all the beans.

Peach Pits

Number of players: small group
Materials needed: six peach pits (or something similar) painted black on one side, medium-size nonbreakable bowl, five beans per player
To play: Place the peach pits in the bowl. One at a time, each player shakes and rolls the peach pits onto the playing surface. If five or more pits of the same color are showing, each player gives the roller one bean. If less than five pits of the same color are showing, no beans are exchanged. The pits are put back in the bowl, and the bowl is passed to the next player. Play continues until one player has all the beans.

Hide the Stone
Number of players: two
Materials needed: small stone, four or five moccasins (use disposable drinking cups)
To play: In turn each player secretly hides the stone under one cup. The other player tries to guess where the stone is hidden.

Which Hand?
Number of players: two
Materials needed: two bones (use small wooden cylinders)—one decorated
To play: In turn each player conceals one cylinder in each hand. The other player tries to guess which hand holds the decorated cylinder.

Keeping the Culture Alive

It is important that students understand that the Native American culture is not only an important part of our country's past—it's an important part of our country's present and future too. The following literature selections introduce students to present-day Native Americans who proudly carry on the heritage of their people.

Red Bird

Written by Barbara Mitchell
Illustrated by Todd L. W. Doney
Lothrop, Lee & Shepard Books; 1996

Today the majority of Nanticoke, an Algonquin tribe, live in southern Delaware. Every September the Nanticoke Indian Association hosts a powwow. Native Americans representing more than 40 tribes come from near and far to join in the singing, dancing, eating of Native American foods, and exhibiting of crafts that characterize this festive occasion. In this magnificent picture book, Katie's present-day story is woven with the history of the Algonquin people as she prepares for and participates in this annual gathering. Luminous oil paintings reveal the heritage of a proud culture.

Cherokee Summer

Written by Diane Hoyt-Goldsmith
Photographed by Lawrence Migdale
Holiday House, Inc.; 1993

Like many other children, ten-year-old Bridget rides a school bus and struggles with her homework. She is also a young girl who is very proud of her Cherokee heritage. In this beautifully photographed volume, Bridget informs readers about the history of the Cherokee people as she describes how she spends her summer doing the things that she enjoys most!

Everglades: Buffalo Tiger and the River of Grass

Written & Photographed by Peter Lourie
Boyds Mills Press, 1994

The author—guided by Buffalo Tiger, the former chief of the Miccosukees—steers readers through the *Pa-hay-okee*, or the Grassy Water, of the Everglades. The special relationship between the Everglades and the Miccosukee Indians is brought to light through the unique perspective of Buffalo Tiger. The ecology of the Everglades and how pollution and overdevelopment threaten this river of grass are explored as well. The singular environment is captured by superior photography.

The Sacred Harvest: Ojibway Wild Rice Gathering

Written by Gordon Regguinti
Photographed by Dale Kakkak
Lerner Publications Company, 1992

For 11-year-old Glen Jackson, Jr., this is the day he has waited for all year! It is the first time his father will take him out to gather *mahnomin*, the sacred food of the Ojibway people. Color photographs and informative text show how Glen learns to harvest the rice on the Bowstring River, then finish the rice at his grandmother's house so that it is ready to cook and eat. Readers discover that families like the Jacksons have been harvesting wild rice for generations—keeping alive an Ojibway tradition.

Additional Resources for Your Woodland Studies

Indians of the Northeast Woodlands

Written by Beatrice Siegel
Illustrated by William Sauts Bock
Walker And Company, 1992

In a simple question-and-answer format, the author helps young readers understand the lifestyle and culture of the Indians of the Northeast Woodlands, past and present. There are also suggestions of places to visit and a list of related books.

The Iroquois: A First Americans Book

Written by Virginia Driving Hawk Sneve
Illustrated by Ronald Himler
Holiday House, Inc.; 1995

In a series of short, simple essays, the lifestyle, history, and convictions of the Iroquois are explained. Generous illustrations offer details of the first Americans' lives including tools, weapons, clothing, transportation, and shelter. Information about present-day Iroquois is included as well. This slim volume is an excellent primary study of the Iroquois.

Homes of the Eastern Woodland Natives

The Algonquins lived in dome-shaped houses. The houses were made from small trees and covered with sheets of bark.

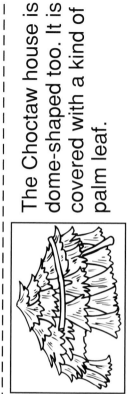

The Iroquois used trees to make their homes. These bark-covered homes were called *longhouses*.

The Cherokee used mud and grass to make dome-shaped houses. Each roof was woven.

The Choctaw house is dome-shaped too. It is covered with a kind of palm leaf.

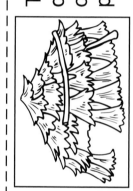

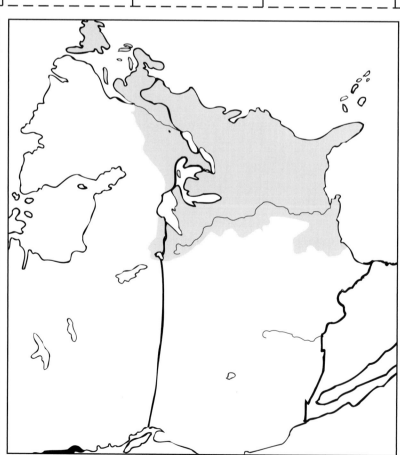

Staple pages here.

More Native American Ideas

A Native American Game

Your students will have fun playing this typical game. Begin with several dried peach pits or pebbles. Mark one side of each. Place pits in four shallow bowls or baskets. Divide your class into four teams. Two teams will compete against the other two. The first player on each team has a bowl with the same number of pits in it.

Play begins as students give the bowl a slight toss to flip the pits into the air. For every pit that lands with the marked side up, one point is scored. The game continues as players take turns. Although Native Americans kept their own score, you may appoint a scorekeeper for each side. The team with the highest score is the winner. It was customary for every member of the winning team to receive a pony from the losing side!

Shell Runtee Pendant

Share with your students that jewelry was used by the Wampanoag for beauty, identification, currency, and ceremonies. Much of the jewelry consisted of beads and adornments made from shells. One particular pendant was called a shell runtee: it was a circular, decorated shell.

Have each student create a replica of a shell runtee pendant. Give each child a foam circle cut from craft foam or a Styrofoam tray. Have each child create a dot design on her circle using colorful fine-tipped permanent markers. When each pendant has been decorated, have each child punch a hole in her pendant and string it on a 26-inch length of yarn to make a necklace. Beautiful!

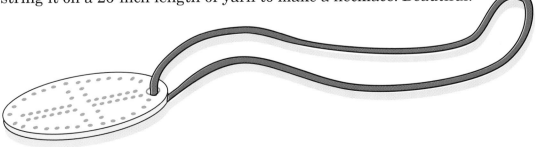

Dreamcatchers

Have students make mini-dreamcatchers from folded paper. To make a dreamcatcher, place a circular tracer atop a folded piece of paper so that one edge of the circle slightly overlaps the fold. Trace; then cut out the resulting shape. Using a hole puncher, punch a hole near the center of the top circle. Using crayons or markers, draw a web and a willow hoop as shown. Inside the folded project, illustrate a good dream that has drifted through the center hole. Sweet dreams!

Totem Poles

Convert empty fabric bolts into inexpensive totem poles to complement your study of Northwest Native Americans. Ask your local fabric stores for fabric bolts they would otherwise discard. Have youngsters decorate them with tagboard scraps, markers, and yarn to create designs that represent the class. Then stack the totem poles to display them outside your classroom door.

Trudy Naddy—Gr. 3
Gladstone, OR

A Look at Dreams

Have youngsters share their sleep visions by making this dreamy bulletin board! Duplicate the framed buckskin below onto tan or white construction paper for each student. Provide colored chalk for your children and have each child create a "Dream-Vision" picture. Spray each completed picture with hairspray to keep the chalk from smearing. Display the completed projects on a bulletin board entitled "Our Dream-Visions."

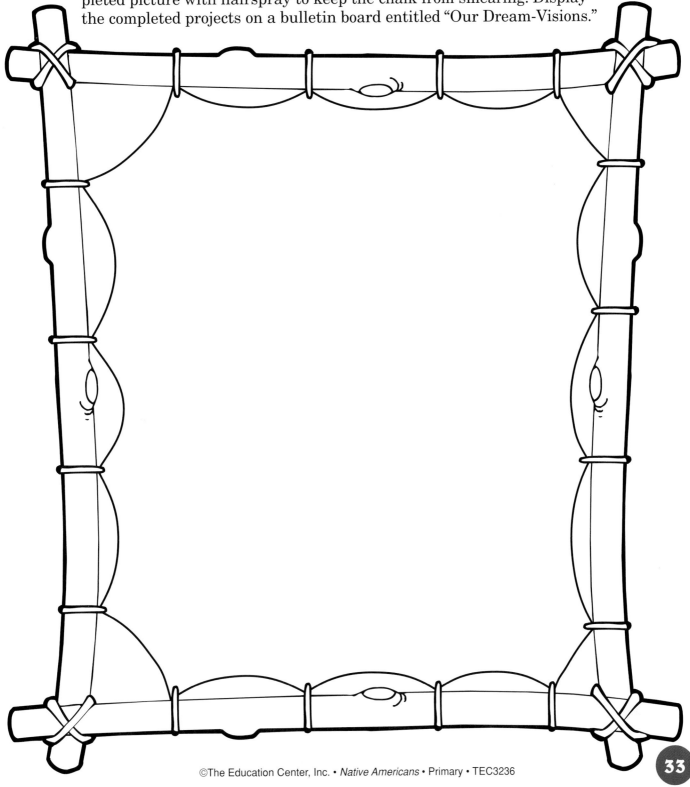

Nature Provides

This activity helps students understand that the air, water, food, and shelter that they need to survive all come from nature. Divide students into small groups and give each group a length of bulletin-board paper bearing a circular outline. Have each group brainstorm what it needs to survive on earth and write the items outside its circle. Inside its circle, the group writes or illustrates the origin of each listed item. For example, the origin of a house might be trees and clay (wood and brick). Then the group draws lines to connect the items to their origins. Help students recognize that each circle is filled with natural resources—gifts from nature.

Wampum

Wampum, purple and white beads made from conch and clam shells, were used by Native Americans as decorations, as a means of identifying a spokesperson, and as money. Native Americans treasured the beads because they were difficult to make. Because white shells were more abundant, purple wampum was worth twice as much as white wampum. The beads were laced together to create wampum belts which usually conveyed a meaning or recorded an event.

Here's how to make wampum in your classroom. Mix red and blue food coloring in water to dye macaroni. Plain macaroni will serve as white wampum. After it dries, use dental floss or string to thread macaroni into jewelry. Give purple wampum a value of 10¢ and white wampum a value of 5¢. Set up a trading post and let students use their wampum to make purchases.

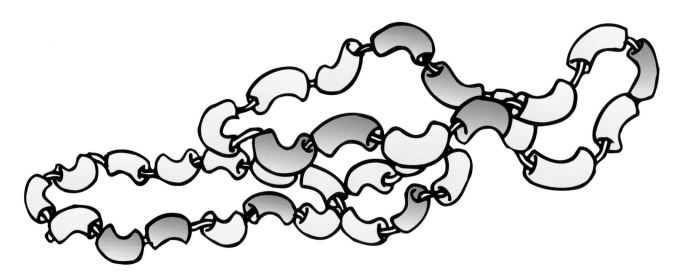

Reproducible Activities...

Note to the Teacher

A study of the first Thanksgiving often leads to discussion of Native Americans who shared in that feast. This unit is designed to present a brief look at the life of the Wampanoag tribe—those who assisted and befriended the English families of Plymouth Colony. If desired, incorporate this unit into a traditional study of the colonists' arrival and the first Thanksgiving celebration.

Materials Needed

Each student will need:
— a copy of page 37
— a pencil or crayon
— a brown, paper lunch bag
— glue

How to Use Page 37

1. Introduce your students to the structure of the Wampanoag home by sharing information from "Background for the Teacher: Wampanoag Native Americans."
2. Distribute page 37 to each student; then guide students in reading about wigwams.
3. Explain that the frame of a wigwam was made from small trees that were bent and tied together. Ask each child to use a pencil or crayon to draw more poles for his wigwam frame.
4. Give each student a paper bag, and ask him to crumple and unfold it. Then have each child tear small pieces (about 1" x 2") from the sack to represent tree bark.
5. Instruct each child to glue several paper-bag pieces atop his wigwam frame.

Background for the Teacher
Wampanoag Native Americans

The Wampanoag tribe inhabited areas of Massachusetts prior to the Pilgrims' arrival. This was one of many Algonquian-speaking tribes of the Eastern Woodlands.

Because of their location, this tribe was the first to encounter European colonists who settled at Plymouth Colony. These Pilgrims met and formed a peace treaty with the Wampanoag in 1621. The peace lasted for more than 50 years, but the increased arrival of Europeans eventually broke down the friendly ties. The Wampanoag's way of life was changed considerably by European influence.

Prior to their encounter with Europeans, the lifestyle of the Wampanoag included many facets of basic survival. The Wampanoag Native Americans lived in homes called *wigwams*. Each home was made by covering a frame of bent saplings with sheets of birch bark or woven grass mats. Homes varied in size depending on the number of people they housed. Small, temporary wigwams were sometimes assembled during hunting season.

Wampanoag travel consisted of two methods. On land they traveled by foot. Sometimes deerskin moccasins were worn for protection. In the winter, snowshoes helped the Wampanoag walk atop deep snow. The Wampanoag also traveled on waterways, and were experts at making canoes. The canoes were crafted using sapling frames, layers of birch bark, and gummy sap as waterproofing.

Much of the Wampanoag's lifestyle was dedicated to hunting, planting, gathering, and fishing for food. They hunted deer, bear, and moose as well as beaver, raccoon, and rabbit. Turkey, duck, and goose were among the fowl that were used as food. Indians also gathered foods from the wild, such as berries, fruits, and nuts. Some of their foods were planted and tended, such as corn, squash, and beans. Another mainstay in the Wampanoag diet was fish.

Clothing was made using materials that were available in nature. Deerskins served as material for many clothing items. Decorative beads were made from shells, and dyes were made from plants.

The Algonquian-speaking tribes—including the Wampanoag—were known for their generally peaceful nature. They established the tradition of *powwows* within their tribes exclusively to promote friendships and good relations. A powwow was defined as a time for feasting, gift giving, singing, dancing, and game playing. The friendship bag was part of the powwow tradition. Indians attending a powwow would take several of these embellished shoulder bags filled with meat or other valued items. Then they would give them to their friends as gifts.

The Wampanoag of today try to find a balance between modern and traditional ways of life. They strive to preserve their rich cultural heritage for younger generations by teaching traditional religious beliefs, ceremonial practices, art forms, and family values. However, their ancestral means of travel, food-gathering practices, and home-building techniques have been replaced by modern-day methods.

Name _____

Building a Home

Some Native Americans lived in **wigwams.**
These houses were made from trees.
Native Americans bent small trees to make frames.
They covered the frames with sheets of bark.

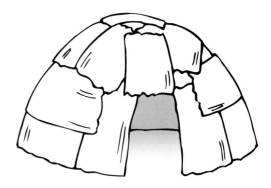

Draw, tear paper, and glue to make a wigwam.

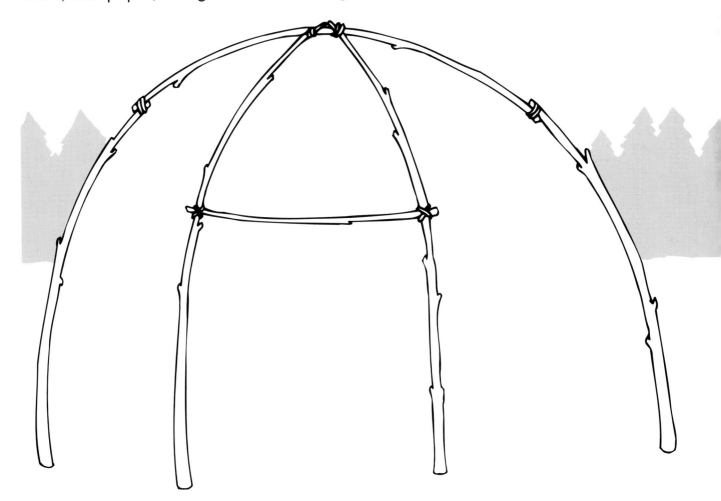

How to Use Page 39

1. Introduce your students to the Wampanoag means of travel by sharing information from "Background for the Teacher: Wampanoag Native Americans" on page 36.

2. Distribute a copy of page 39 to each student; then guide students in reading about Native American travel.

3. Instruct each child to cut out the pictures at the bottom of the page.

4. Help students read each transportation method or aid in bold print.

5. Ask each child to glue a picture in each square to match each word.

6. Have him draw a line from each picture to the location where each transportation method would be used.

Name _____

Getting Around

Native Americans used **canoes** to travel on rivers.
The canoes were made from tree bark.
Native Americans walked on land.
Sometimes they wore **moccasins** on their feet.
They used **snowshoes** to help them walk on snow.

Cut and glue to match.
Draw a line to show where each would be used.

moccasins	

canoe	

snowshoes	

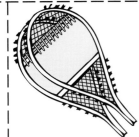    

39

The Legend of the Indian Paintbrush

How to Use Pages 41–45

Read the book *The Legend of the Indian Paintbrush* by Tomie dePaola to your class. Lead your students in a discussion about the story. Then duplicate pages 41, 43, and 44 for each of your students to complete.

Background for the Teacher

Plains Indians

The Native Americans referred to as the Plains Indians included many different tribes. These tribes lived in a similar region of the country and they shared, to some extent, a similar way of life. Languages among the Plains Indians differed from tribe to tribe. Some of the Plains Indians are listed below.

— **The Pawnee** farmed *maize* (Indian corn) and were located west of the Missouri River in the area we now call Nebraska.

— **The Sauk and Fox** lived together as a single tribe in the Iowa area. They lived in dome-shaped huts covered with birch bark, rushes, or mats.

— **The Mandan** lived in the Missouri River/ Dakota territory. They farmed and hunted for their food and clothing. They lived in sturdy, round earthen huts. They lived near the river and made boats called *bullboats* by stretching buffalo hides over wooden frames.

— **The Osage** lived in areas of Arkansas, Missouri, and Oklahoma. They were hunters.

— **The Iroquois** lived in the area east of the Great Lakes and were mainly farmers.

— **The Sioux** were hunters and nomads who lived in the South Dakota area. Their homes were tents called *teepees,* which were easily moved from place to place.

Before the horse was introduced as an animal for riding, some of the Plains Indians hunted buffalo in wolf disguises. The hunters covered themselves in wolf skins and moved toward a herd. Buffalo usually did not run from wolves, which allowed the hunters to move close to the buffalo and shoot several arrows. In this manner, they were able to obtain the meat and hides needed for their existence.

Answer Key

1. The wise **shaman** spoke to Little Gopher.
   — medicine man   — father

2. An Indian **maiden** came out of the clouds.
   — young lady   — colt

3. Little Gopher saw his **vision** in the sky.
   — face   — something seen in a dream

4. Little Gopher painted a white **buckskin.**
   — soft leather   — sheet

5. Little Gopher **longed** to share his Dream-Vision.
   — wished   — decided

6. The **warriors** brought animal skins back from the hunt.
   — leaders   — fighting men

7. Little Gopher found the colors he was **seeking.**
   — stirring   — looking for

8. Little Gopher painted pictures of the warriors' **deeds.**
   — acts of courage   — land

9. The hill was **ablaze** with color.
   — glowing   — surrounded by

10. The brushes **multiplied** into many plants.
    — mixed   — increased in number

11. The hills and meadows **burst** into bloom.
    — appeared suddenly   — started

12. Little Gopher followed the **customs** of his tribe.
    — usual habits   — trails

Pick a Paintbrush

Read each sentence.
Choose the correct meaning of the bold word as it
  is used in the story.
Color the paintbrush.

1. The wise **shaman** spoke to Little Gopher.

   medicine man   father

2. An Indian **maiden** came out of the clouds.

   young lady   colt

3. Little Gopher saw his **vision** in the sky.

   face   something seen in a dream

4. Little Gopher painted a white **buckskin.**

   soft leather   sheet

5. Little Gopher **longed** to share his Dream-Vision.

   wished   decided

6. The **warriors** brought animal skins back from the hunt.

   leaders   fighting men

7. Little Gopher found the colors he was **seeking.**

   stirring   looking for

8. Little Gopher painted pictures of the warriors' **deeds.**

   acts of courage   land

9. The hill was **ablaze** with color.

   glowing   surrounded by

10. The brushes **multiplied** into many plants.

    mixed   increased in number

11. The hills and meadows **burst** into bloom.

    appeared suddenly   started

12. Little Gopher followed the **customs** of his tribe.

    usual habits   trails

---

Bonus Box: On the back of this sheet, color a picture of a beautiful sunset.

Background for the Teacher
Tomie dePaola

Tomie dePaola (de-*pow*-la) is among the most prolific authors of self-illustrated children's books. He says he made the decision to become an artist and author of books when he was four. After graduating from Pratt Institute in 1956, dePaola spent six months in a Benedictine monastery where he says he was "sort of the resident artist." About his art style, dePaola says, "...I'm drawn to Romanesque and folk art. I think that my style is very close to those—very simple and direct. I simplify." Tomie dePaola says his dream is to have one of his books touch some individual child and change that child's life for the better.

Tomie dePaola Booklist

The Art Lesson (Putnam Publishing Group, 1989)
Bill and Pete (Putnam Publishing Group, 1978)
The Cloud Book (Holiday House, Inc.; 1975)
Fin M'Coul, the Giant of Knockmany Hill (Holiday House, Inc.; 1981)
The Legend of Old Befana (Harcourt Brace Jovanovich, 1980)
The Legend of the Bluebonnet (Retold by Tomie dePaola, Putnam Publishing Group, 1983)
Nana Upstairs and Nana Downstairs (Puffin Books, 1978)
Now One Foot, Now the Other (Putnam Publishing Group, 1981)
Pancakes for Breakfast (Harcourt Brace Jovanovich, 1978)
The Popcorn Book (Holiday House, Inc.; 1978)
Strega Nona (Simon & Schuster Trade, 1979)
Watch Out for the Chicken Feet in Your Soup (Simon & Schuster Trade, 1974)

Name _____

Links of a Legend

Write one story event on each strip.

glue

The Legend of the Indian Paintbrush
by Tomie dePaola

Name _____

glue
_____
_____

glue
_____
_____

glue
_____
_____

glue
_____
_____

glue
_____
_____

glue
_____
_____

Make a story chain.
Cut out the strips.
Glue the strips in order like a chain.
Start with the title.

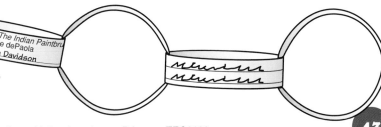

The Legend Of The Indian Paintbru
by Tomie dePaola
Name_____ Eva Davidson

Design a Sign

Make a sign that could be placed near a field of Indian Paintbrushes.
On the sign, retell the legend of the Indian Paintbrush so that visitors will know how
  this plant received its name.

_____
Sign Title

_____

_____

_____

_____

_____

_____

_____

_____

Sign Maker _____

Bonus Box: Draw a picture of your favorite flower on the back of this sheet. Below the picture, write a legend about how the flower got its name.

Name _____

Favorite Foods

Native Americans got food from the land.
They hunted animals like deer.
They gathered foods like fruit.
They planted foods like corn.
They also caught fish.

Word Bank

pumpkins	deer		corn	fish
maple sap	goose	duck	nuts	fruit
	beans			

Circle each word.
Use the word bank.

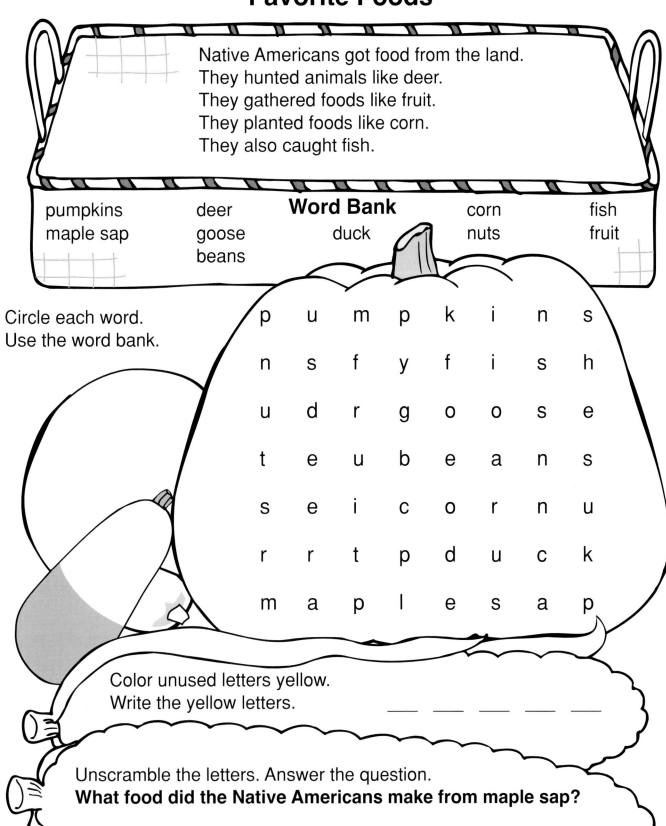

p	u	m	p	k	i	n	s
n	s	f	y	f	i	s	h
u	d	r	g	o	o	s	e
t	e	u	b	e	a	n	s
s	e	i	c	o	r	n	u
r	r	t	p	d	u	c	k
m	a	p	l	e	s	a	p

Color unused letters yellow.
Write the yellow letters. ___ ___ ___ ___ ___

Unscramble the letters. Answer the question.
What food did the Native Americans make from maple sap?

___ ___ ___ ___ ___ ___

Bonus Box:
On the back of this sheet, draw something you eat with this food today.

45

Materials Needed for Each Student

— copy of page 47
— crayons or markers
— scissors
— glue

How to Use Page 47

1. Share with your youngsters some background information about Native American Day (see "Background for the Teacher").
2. Remind students that Native Americans were our country's very first Americans. Explain that Native Americans shared many wonderful things with the people who later came to live in North America. As a class read aloud the information on page 47. Then ask each child to color and cut out the pictures at the bottom of the page.
3. Read aloud the following descriptions. After each description allow time for students to glue the matching picture in the appropriate location.
   — Native Americans used this for food. They introduced this food to the Pilgrims. Today we call it *corn*. Native Americans called it *maize*. Glue the picture of maize in square E.
   — This special boat was invented by Native Americans. It was made by hollowing out a tree. Glue the picture of the canoe in square H.
   — Many Native Americans used these to hunt and kill animals for food. Native Americans only killed what they could eat. Glue the picture of the bow and arrow in square A.
   — Thanks to Native Americans, we have shoes that enable a person to walk on top of very deep snow. Glue the picture of the snowshoes in square J.
   — Native American men and women wove beautiful baskets. Into some, they wove shells and feathers. These were used to carry water, seeds, and grains. Glue the picture of the baskets in square C.
   — Native Americans used the earth's clay to make pottery containers. Some were for

everyday use. Others were only used for special occasions and ceremonies. Glue the picture of the pottery in square F.
   — Bones, clay, beads, leather, shells, and many other items were used to make beautiful pieces of jewelry. Glue the picture of the jewelry in square I.
   — Native Americans used soft animal leather to create footwear. Glue the picture of the moccasins in square B.
   — Though we often use it differently today than Native Americans did long ago, this object was created by the first Americans. Glue the picture of the toboggan in square G.
   — This one-person boat was made by stretching animal skins over a wooden frame. Glue the picture of the kayak in square D.
4. Invite students to work together to complete the Bonus Box activity.

Background for the Teacher
Native American Day

Native American Day is dedicated to recognizing and honoring the contributions of North America's Native Americans. It is neither a religious nor a ceremonial occasion, but rather an educational and promotional event designed to increase the awareness of the accomplishments of Native Americans. Because Native American Day is not a universal holiday in the United States, its observation varies from state to state. However, many states choose to observe Native American Day on the fourth Friday of September.

Answer Key
Top row: bow and arrow, moccasins, baskets, kayak, maize
Bottom row: pottery, toboggan, canoe, jewelry, snowshoes

A.	B.	C.	D.	E.

NATIVE AMERICAN GIFTS

Native Americans have lived in America for a very long time. They were living in America before Columbus arrived. Native Americans are a very important part of our country's history. Find out about some of the things that Native Americans shared with people who came to America to live.

Listen carefully.
Follow the directions.

Bonus Box: These are only a few of the many things that Native Americans shared with new Americans. Can you think of others? Can you think of ways that Native Americans share their knowledge and talents today?

F.	G.	H.	I.	J.

baskets	maize	bow and arrow	kayak	toboggan
snowshoes	jewelry	canoe	moccasins	pottery

Telling Tales

Some stories tell about the world.
What does each story tell about?
Cut and paste.

I am yellow.
I am sweet.
I am good to eat.

I can help.
I can run fast.
You can ride on me.

I am fast.
I am shy.
I can run away.

I am hot.
I give light.
I am far away.

 corn the sun  a deer  a horse